THE SCARIEST PLACES ON EARTH
THE BONE CHAPEL

BY NICK GORDON

TORQUE
™

BELLWETHER MEDIA · MINNEAPOLIS, MN

Are you ready to take it to the extreme?
Torque books thrust you into the action-packed world
of sports, vehicles, mystery, and adventure. These
books may include dirt, smoke, fire, and chilling tales.
WARNING : read at your own risk.

Library of Congress Cataloging-in-Publication Data

Gordon, Nick.
 The bone chapel / by Nick Gordon.
     pages cm. -- (Torque : the scariest places on earth)
 Includes bibliographical references and index.
 Summary: "Engaging images accompany information about the Bone Chapel. The combination of high-
interest subject matter and light text is intended for students in grades 3 through 7"--Provided by publisher.
 ISBN 978-1-60014-946-7 (hardcover: alk. paper)
 1. Ossuaries--Czech Republic--Sedlec Region--Juvenile literature. 2. Human remains (Archaeology)--
Czech Republic--Sedlec Region--Juvenile literature. 3. Sedlec Region (Czech Republic)--Antiquities--
Juvenile literature. I. Title.
 GT3271.C9G67 2014
 393'.1094371--dc23
                                                                      2013008944

This edition first published in 2014 by Bellwether Media, Inc.

Printed in the United States of America, North Mankato, MN.

TABLE OF CONTENTS

CHAPTER 1

SURROUNDED BY SKULLS

A small **chapel** stands before you. From the outside, it seems like an ordinary church. As you step inside, you see that it is anything but ordinary. The walls, the ceiling, and everything inside are covered in bones. The dead are all around you!

A chill runs up your spine. Skulls stare down at you from the walls. A **chandelier** of bones hangs from the ceiling. Ropes of bones dangle overhead. Welcome to the Sedlec **Ossuary**, also known as the Bone Chapel!

CHAPTER 2

BASEMENT OF BONES

The Bone Chapel sits in the small Czech Republic town of Kutná Hora. Before 1278, there was nothing special about this place. It was home to a small **abbey** and a **cemetery**. Then the local **abbot** took a trip to the **Holy Land**. He brought back some soil.

The abbot sprinkled the soil over the cemetery. Word spread that the cemetery had holy soil. People from all over Central Europe wanted to be buried there. The cemetery grew. Then a terrible **plague** called the Black Death swept through Europe. The dead kept coming.

The cemetery was getting bigger and bigger. Around 1400, a church was built on the cemetery grounds. Workers had to dig up many graves during construction. They piled the bones in the chapel beneath the church.

Over the years, new bodies filled the cemetery. Old bones were placed in the chapel to make more room. It became a giant **crypt**!

CHAPTER 3

A DARK BEAUTY

In 1870, woodworker František Rint was hired to arrange the bones. He created the Bone Chapel we know today. Rint lined the walls with bones. He strung them together and let them swoop from the ceiling. He even created two giant **chalices** out of leg and hip bones.

chalice

The chapel's most famous feature is its bone chandelier. Rint used every bone in the human body to create it. The chandelier hangs in the center of the room. On certain days, its candles are lit. The flickering flames cast skeletal shadows throughout the chapel.

Rint also built four huge bell-shaped mounds of bones. One stands in each corner of the chapel. He crafted a creepy **coat of arms** for the local family that hired him. He decorated an **altar** with skulls. Then he signed his work in bone!

František Rint's signature

CHAPEL OF BONES

Portugal's Capela dos Ossos is another church decorated with bones. Its walls are lined with the skeletons of about 5,000 people.

coat of arms

DRAWN TO DEATH

About 200,000 people visit the Bone Chapel each year.

Today, **tourists** travel far to see the Bone Chapel. Many report a strong feeling of death in the place. They note a strange energy within the chapel walls. But most only notice its haunting beauty. Do spirits of the dead linger inside the chapel? If so, are they searching for peace?

GLOSSARY

abbey—a place where monks or nuns live and pray

abbot—the head of an abbey

altar—a table or flat stone block used as the center of a religious ceremony

cemetery—a place where the dead are buried

chalices—goblets or formal drinking cups

chandelier—a decorative hanging light with branches for light bulbs or candles

chapel—a small building used for prayer and religious services

coat of arms—a picture or symbol used to represent a family name

crypt—a sealed room used to store human remains

Holy Land—a region in the Middle East that Jews, Christians, and Muslims consider sacred

ossuary—a container or room that holds the bones of dead people

plague—a deadly, fast-spreading disease

tourists—people who travel to visit another place

TO LEARN MORE

AT THE LIBRARY

Arnold, Caroline. *Your Skeletal System*. Minneapolis, Minn.: Lerner Publications Co., 2013.

Hawkins, John. *Hauntings*. New York, N.Y.: PowerKids Press, 2012.

Simmons, Walter. *The Czech Republic*. Minneapolis, Minn.: Bellwether Media, Inc., 2012.

ON THE WEB

Learning more about the Bone Chapel is as easy as 1, 2, 3.

1. Go to www.factsurfer.com.

2. Enter "Bone Chapel" into the search box.

3. Click the "Surf" button and you will see a list of related Web sites.

With factsurfer.com, finding more information is just a click away.

INDEX